CHARM

CHARM

CHRISTINE MCNAIR

BookThug 2017

The production of this book was made possible through the
generous assistance of the Canada Council for the Arts and the
Ontario Arts Council. BookThug also acknowledges the support
of the Government of Canada through the Canada Book Fund
and the Government of Ontario through the Ontario Book
Publishing Tax Credit and the Ontario Book Fund.

Library and Archives Canada Cataloguing in Publication

McNair, Christine, 1978–, author
        Charm / Christine McNair. — First edition.

Poems.
Issued in print and electronic formats.
ISBN 978-1-77166-318-2 (SOFTCOVER)
ISBN 978-1-77166-319-9 (HTML)
ISBN 978-1-77166-320-5 (PDF)
ISBN 978-1-77166-321-2 (KINDLE)

        I. Title.

PS8625.N33 C53 2017   C811'.6   C2017-900738-6
                                       C2017-900739-4

PRINTED IN CANADA

For Rose and Aoife

Something gathers up
the fragments, and
nothing is lost.
— Fourcrois' Chemistry

contents

THE PROBLEM OF ORCHIDS

I

The orchid has large, waxy white, star-like flowers with a pronounced lip and a foot-long spur that projects from the back of the flower. Since this white orchid had a strong spicy fragrance at night, Darwin hypothesized that it must be pollinated by a nocturnal hawk moth with a proboscis (a tongue) that extended to 12 inches.

2

deviant strokework nipple heavy
gagged threshwork needle stuck

hand punched fretwork
distressed countenance skullwork
affect all sense of proportion

I can't say it so I'll say it slant

3

muscles of the human body: neck: platysma:
draws the corners of the mouth inferiorly and widens it
(as in expressions of sadness and fright) also draws
the skin of the neck superiorly when teeth are clenched

4

In the orchid, the pollinia attached itself by a stalk or extension that is hygroscopic (meaning it bends when moisture levels or the levels of humidity change). Once dry, the pollinia is in perfect position to attach to the stigma.

5

in a room in a house in a
basement something borrowed something blue
cplus cans blossom

a copse of flowers
cross-referenced
pepper skin

veil invested blueblood seed pearl
sticky

here's at it then:

fingers tighten in lulls ears
say: *mine mine* minion
miniature minaret tower

rapunzel rapunzel
let down your hair

6

How many of these questions do you answer YES:
Are you afraid of your orchid? · Do you sometimes
feel like you have to walk on pins and needles to keep
your orchid from getting angry? · Has your orchid
ever hit, slapped, choked or pushed you? · Has your
orchid ever pulled your hair? · Do you feel like you
deserve to be punished? · Does your orchid drive you
crazy or make you feel like you're going crazy? · Have
you believed that your orchid would kill you? · Have
you been told by your orchid that he or she would
kill you? · Has your orchid threatened or attempted
to commit suicide? · Have you been forced by your
orchid to do something you didn't want to do? · Do
you feel emotionally numb? · Have you ever left
your orchid because of how you were treated, but
later returned, or allowed your orchid to return, after
promises that it would "all be different?"

impetuous temptation and motel sick stopovers
our products of conception
defy gravity

mouth breeds insolent print
splendor of letters and brace of doves
bent counter clockwise slept

fluorescent with the patron saint
of lost causes divinity lessons

see: bitework craftwork crewelwork piecework
bitwork clockwork brushwork bodywork
cabinetwork firework framework
meshwork ironwork legwork stonework

8

lethality guide: frequent increase severe
escalate threat escalate frequent intoxicate
increase force threat impair weapon stress
violence a new relationship for either

9

as far as orchids are concerned –
we have known for a long time that they are
notoriously promiscuous –

still

I am not your dove
for safekeeping.

MATERIA

materia prima

An inflection of slowness – that is to say, to believe that
the obscure is accurate – is the base material the prima obscura

a hand appears then vanishes, obstructs
the base material

run through method, through practice
through patience and impatience through slow revolving
it is only ever the hands

either you have them or you don't
and there's no revelation more tender

intention

"hand made" techno-centric culture making
things by hand a full circle phenomenon
hand made cycled through the processed the
manufactured the markers of progress the
impact

human activities nature our attention

= pre-tech practices preserving
at irrevocable cost
the hands of craftspeople

my original intention:
a bellows
a new world

in matia

est matia
est surum
sure-est

the bookbinder
the bowmaker
the dressmaker
the jeweller

see:
bookbinder's limp
arthritis
metal lung

or:
seamstress's cramp
stonemaker's lung
teamaker's asthma
thresher's fever
vanillism
washerwoman's itch
weaver's bottom
woolsorter's disease
zinc chills

that is:
bookbinder's cramp
dressmaker's pleurisy
bowmaker's ague
jeweller's hump

□

slant view broken (made) endbands abraded edge diagonal plough
line green cloth or leather sides sluiced pages missing board broken
shoulders falling lonely paper spine lining bent rounding swerves
wear patterns

head or tail indistinguished
endband cracks midway
cries a little

distinguishes
wear and tear

a bloom pear flush grain patterns
what rubbed boards say about the rubbing

commercial
late 19th to early 20th
cusp edge
predatory squares

imply the work of hands
the craftworks the bill of sale
a rumple in the timeframe

□□

*fixed measure scratched vertical 7 8 9 10 slant downward bars
crenulations imperfect scoring*

scored impermeable indirect obtain surrender
develop carve out
impair fully

the futility of metal objects
and the awkwardness of their
permanence

pile of bows supposes wood measures a grey flat surface wear marks
a collapsed pile of canes tilted heads somehow sea horses

lyrical low music side tilts, collapses
low lying bridges, parsed and swept
what seems like potential a falling down
mournful pull over stringwork

Jacqueline du Pré caresses cello
pours Elgar at two tears a second

sweet wine and a cup half measured
= her weep of it

a cut out bow a mould a patterned straight grained wood an absence
a cut away a portion a loss an echo a shadow

in place of a song a gasp an echo a tune to walk into
the gape gapes it gawps it gulls it grows
blue pieces a place to throw things a void in space
we fall into we fall backward there's no supposing

the void beckons beguiles demands
fingers

the violin it is the bow:
l'archet

milky threads swirling rounded bend individual linework hair
forest smooth violet violence violin dips and waves

Siberian horse cowers the flank twitches
a bulbous palm to the shank
the bleached pace of light

expression of tenor upon
the maker's face it is all in the asking
in the Конский волос

the blue blooded petulance
of hanked tones

what? gelatine glue wax resin adhesive stooped figure sad
accumulation rumpled skirts bending blob penance

sick antique yellow cross-linked

the glue pot swallowed
collaborates with wicked hooves

apprentices are slow
to catch right meaning

this brat on the border,
burbled resin or wax

watch this sloth eye
caress its maker

thin wood shavings worms tracework lying over felts undisguised
landscapes sea creatures fuzzy grey warmth pale warming roses

wood planed soft

smells warm and

salted feels silk to

callused fingers

bowmaker in studio tools glue lamp magnifier stoop pressure
downward clutter abandoned bits sneak open of a drawer no eyes
no face

       rehairing
       cambering
       wraps and grips

       bow tip in the french style
       gold mounted snakewood german d bass bow

       pernambuco

       preservation
       restoration
       sustainability

       much later:

       such flow in the phrasing
       sound's really quite fine

two sparkles on white background dots in parallel curve of hip pool
of wet

beauty sleeps cries fights beasts
sucks several gorgeous
wet tears off painted nail or clutch

such flush saint sweetness of ribbon tied
round the throat a full heart a cupful

pinched stitches gentle
satin swell luminous
peel across a white tincture

alien pins clustered pinned into textile blue background grey textile
mushroom shine of pins

colonies on carefully studied
loops and bends filtered
hemlines and strictures

delineated tracery white
balustrades

a pinch of concentration
at the brow

threaded metal sewing machine cool absence of hole degraded
thread flyaway disappearing left pooled metal open frankenstein

wide eyes of
needle sympathetic and gullible
a stitch of fuschia reigns

believe in stitches (they're quaint)
and pivot silver sailed white wash
apprentices with milky cheeks

they slip under the pale corner of a docket
translucent apparel of a ledger
a bill of sale

increased haphazard cluster of pills dots of light rough wool
textile fuzzy pins in background misty mushrooms dots of light
uncertainties memory loss of purpose time

washed blue what colour's in it

the mineral swept browns and
sweet grey love of old

stars predict blood
in every profession

worn metal multicoloured bench fire residue meeting in the middle
dinosaurs graceful neck poignant bend worn sooth

tweezers graze bend and pinch
annealed circumstances dictate
caution we heat and then more heat
and then a cooling and then
we and then we just and then
we are so literally warmed

cogs pins inner workings of a longines watch metal makers marks
serial numbers delicate sprogs wheels clock face without hands

precision cogs up the works
this prick hole next to never
these measures belonging nowhere

how many hours are there
in clock watch fob sprung
wheels pale nailbeds

wild mushrooms chimney sweeps rotating pie plate trees out of focus
greys blues distance loneliness of two portrait of a married couple

one smudge undoes
a real resolute fella
an impassioned civil servant

flurry of wires and saints
collected into pretty girl frocks

fluked light eye shadow and blue-
paned glass each turns a chin

serenades polish and lustre
gorgeous patina grin

collection of files tools missiles warheads steeples wear marks tilted
angles towers round warm head of brass

sing a song for
thinning the dips between
precise silver filaments
stunned short and flat
for pitch-black alloy alluvial

prints push the boundaries
of compressed pores
warm ore fleck stone
gets caught touch tricked
pulled under the smell of metal

on skin the precise perfume
one over another

copper levers rotations circles gears lines uncertainties central pivot
moving pieces blur

tools are extension of hands
of impulses movements

will pulls forward sweet latent
movement, wear marks

chelated advent deep
signature heavy – a bump
to the noggin a graze
to the complet

all our things
dog-eared hazed scratched

impoverished
imperfect
nostalgic
sainted
brutish
short

FRET

all kinds of quiet

throw bolts to the wind and butter my shoulders
do not make me come over there

It is dangerous to chew string or to bite cotton instead
        of taking scissors to it, for, if swallowed, string or
        cotton might wind round your heart and kill you

fishing wire wrapped against peach
bruise heavy collapsing firmaments

a distressing lack of totems boats umbrellas
wrong suit wrong tie wrong elbow wrong mouth wrong wrench

trench

I've forgotten how not to war.
My lines draw blood. I sip trickle.

I'll attest that I always drop
down fall down sleep like
owls unravel my knits

clambering over the engine
I can feel my legs chatter

Discuss discuss discuss

Repetitive strain injury flocks
my satellite mind

I've forgotten peacetime
treaties re-arrange fight me
god damn you fight me

I don't know how to be
anything but a valkyrie

valkyric holler

fatalism

I can see through lead
all the braided contortions
of whosits whatsits

each dim tucked presence
and differentiated sarcomas

satellite minds the clutch
of two sticks rubbed raw

Cassandra at the gate
flouts disarmament

a suffusion of pleasures
in peace time

utterly dissolute blood sorbet
my pumpernickel heart
croons

upon a time

there were three cats a maiden
plus a muddling mess of good and bad

supposing we had something to say then
we might be saying it but

because we don't we merely keep
writing in some semblance of something

some felt scratch kitsch of kirsch and kick

the recording of musical mouse and many
skulled pheasants all askew is renegaded

there's dust mice in the mouth
corners of every soft spoken shell
shocked hellion

sweetness

a dolce tiramisu cut into shreds
reshaped into threats

the trauma of being everywhere
and nowhere all at once

'even when we are quite alone'
'we recognize the same influence'
'a man cannot prevent past impressions'

a desolation of cupcakes and sherry

my ears melt into pads of cotton
wool fear a seed stitch picked off hems

icing sugar caulks broke tile dusts
breast petals fall in drifts

"to fret thy soul with crosses and with cares"

I.
interspliced – my fingers lick
dashboard drip syrup lose venue

slip diagonal beneath
stringed instruments

soft sand sucks toes
black bays my hips
tilt to the wash of it

shoe blunt with beach
my perpetual chafe of

wet

2.
fae folk require raw cherries
devilish red my sticky
goblins

3.
shoulder span cool
stone sweet there's
no ocean where there's
no ocean no ocean

my tongue coasts

4.
beloved bellatrix
beautiful belladonna
flash fictions

5.
my heart's root hem lonely
sweet room murmur

river left wanting

leave bitemarks deep in shoulder flecked
fixed taxologies

mine eye stuck for crossing
cross-paralytics all armour full flesh

you deck me then cross the ways guts

diagonal decked from here to high heaven
supposed something hybrid

dull license of marital machines
cog wheel and sprocket dead centre

bruise rents an armful of banned books
black severance schema suckled

retrospective blur bad floods keep
your hands off me

frenzy

all I can hear is the pitch
of my own sticky pulse
flattened ovoid the push
still thick ever sharp all
I can see is swells of rag
and bone men our collected
works two pounds a penny
each for each all I can taste
is wool plunge cold in river
weeds sketchy aftertaste
of beneficial mud all I can
smell is dazed lilac a wrench
of oversweet saline eyes
crunched onto silk all I can
feel is circled throat cordite
tether lacked safety net
incensed sense of supposed
somewheres craved colour
body curls inwards fierce
folded spiral smallest small

advanced mourning

I bury my mother more times
than not my lover my ex lover
my father my cat

yanking them up and out of the ground
burbly red in their warning in their spectrum
in the developing film canister
or pixel

pixel pixels, I make my life a pixel

a lover, what's the word lover
I hate the word lover I hate
the name and its clumsy sweat

I stymie judgement   progressive enclosures and debt requirements
the length of a kiss – dull issue – depth studies

here's me in my neck of the woods

sunning myself against all odds
across an acreage of concrete

REEL

a

A smudge of red ochre cracked. Leaf after leaf as big as my head. Yellows reds oranges pinks browns. Underfoot, they murmur. I step on them to hear the crackle. Smoke pervades, woodsmoke, leafsmoke, barbeque smoke. The lights carry dried leaves in the shade, pressed botanicals. I pick up leaves with my brother for the Thanksgiving table centrepiece. The smell of turkey and stuffing. Cranberry stains along my dress.

b

My cousin Elisabeth in the woods behind the house, her hair to her hips, or I thought it was. Brushing her hair, sitting on a rock, I hover, worshipfully. She statues, mermaid, siren of the trees, long brown curls and long limbs. Her brothers and my brothers break-up our forest hutch. I turn furious and swear at them, a world too old for my mouth. They gape. First sense of fiery. Righteous indignation. Sword weighed.

c

A paddleboat in the lake, knees kicking.

Straddling the windsurfing board, and Pascale showing me
how. Conscious of my thighs. 10. Love the heft of the bar on
the sail. Leaning into the curve, cutting across the lake. The
deck. Losing my contact in the water. Having to find new
contacts somehow. Somehow. Some translation problem. What
age? Adulthood.

The uneven move of the deck, the dock that is, wobble back.
The small craft hooked to the side. The tiny fishes in grey water.
The fishes. The weeds we'd swim away from. The tickle of the
fishes. Long ago, my waterwings. Puffy brave upper arms.
Popeyed.

d

My mother's dramatic bob, her lips. Watching raccoons cross the road, lolling curved walks, bouncing, large. Little masks and eyes.

Fondue and crackling hot oil, raclette, the importance of not saying 'raclette' as it aggravated my brother. The importance of saying 'raclette'.

e

The sky opening up, family beneath, walking walking over
the lawn, white sheets of something fluttering and crinkling,
growing across the black sky, obscuring the sky, fanning out.
Moving, unknown, fright, beauty. Unknown. Northern Lights?
Unknown.

f

Rock moves. Rock watches the grass. Rock watches the sprinklers.

The lawn long and yellow, burnt at the ridge. The lawn long and green, sprinkler infested. Perfect quarter inch blades. There's a guy.

Satellite swans. I have no TV at home. Yet.

I cloister. I haven. Weep. Sleep in the basement, under earth, cold.

I cloister. Naked in the hot tub and the yawling gaping moon, monstrous silver disk. Stars. And more stars. The wind rushes through leaves. They bustle.

h

prologue:
fish water fish muck water doll statue eel water jellyfish coral
fish seaweed water salt breasts

premise:
fishgirl boy othergirl pause dumbgirl boy prettygirl dumbboy
doomgirl foam

cliff notes:
shipwreck lifesaver bargain tongue dogbed heart weapon ship
waves

interior (her):
gurgle

interior (him):
what?

g

profiled women in small cylindrical frames
sticking their nails into the wood
layers of candy bar wrappers slicked onto hodge podge, blue ribbons
a silvery grey sheen across
there's nothing but names and comments
avatars to follow

icon of the virgin

i

She tries to remember the door's access code, the impulse in the nail, the thread through the darned needle, the blank bucket stare. All of it emeshes, flattens, becomes a study in merged colour.

Her fingers touch porcelain. They curve round the base. Porcelain. Pig vagina. Between two fingers and so slippery.

The smacked up sentence of it pulls over and around and blushes and she clutches and then Thomas opens the door and there's so much whooshing. Flaps of cotton shirt around her face, then yelling, sirens. The blood in it, on it.

Posters embellish. Fray at edge, unwind, come into threads of knits and kites.

A small crayfish. Red in the pond.

She outlines her hand in gold pen, embellishes. It seems larger. Larks at the window.

Invigoration. Vigour.

j

Hospital bed hovers, maintains two inches from the floor. Her mother's pained expressed at her left side, holds hand. She floats. The air contextualizes turns to water then to wine then to water again. Her hair ebbs out around her, grows swirled and reflective. The bed lifts higher and those at bedside rumple and round out and remain backwards and forwards and upside down every and. Round and round curlicue. A soft hollow sound in the ears, the taste of salt on her lips, her ocean. The bed hits the ground with a clatter of springs and metal and water whooshes outwards and out the door and floods the children's playroom, entirely. Two dehumidifiers and a fan.

k

The pleasure and secret of maps under the driver's seat. To pour over and search through. McGonnell's Jump. Lilac Station. Windsor News. Rabbit Fence. Rose Prickle. Secret Lake Sudden Service Lovesick Lake Pen and Ink Margin. Ragu Green. Blood and Roses.

I

A dull bookshelf, plywood with veneer. A scattering of lit titles, mostly business texts, inspirational biographies, 'humour'. Plucked titles to feed her poems. Raw floods tempered under seventies/eighties flowy cotton. Carribean coloured jackets. She digs her nails into the spines, leaves an impression.

m

When she met him she was a garden. When she met him she was linen starched and white. When she met him she was in a pale blue nightdress. When she met him it was nine in the morning. When she met him she smelled of lemons and peach. When she met him her ears were full of dust.

She was full of dust.

When she met him it was dusk and then dark and then dusk again. His limbs marionette and pivot at the joints, they come undone and swerve into themselves. He jaw clatters.

n

A belly expands and contracts.
Up end the blue circle. A table full of marbles.

o

I write my way out of a paper bag. We surrender, evolve,
surrender, evolve, surrender.

p

Dread pitches itself black against the thin of her forearm.
Concaves a visible crease. A flesh of white turns whiter, the
hairs attend. Flex flick flex flick.

Disaster politics make it possible for the impossible and then it
comes up by ten and we're reckless with it, maybe.

q

She anticipates dreads waits supposes surrenders evolves.

pleasantries and other misdemeanours
or notes to a marriage

Impulse heavy
prêt politesse it might
just be that i love you
unscathed

despite of
instead of

thick heavy writes praise
and praises and blue grey
eye blink lip twist and silly owl,

an eye expands
to fit a circle, the bone in
my head quivers

*

Dear darling, I woke this
morning and my fat finger
bone was stuck in the wall

Dear darling, tonight I cluck
my tongue and serrate the
air surrender pitches

Dear darling, a wife's duties
incur penalties. Blinkered and broke
we compose alone

I sleep i.e. dream perchance but not
dip my toes in lead and roll the
baby toe forward. Scent the metal
with lavender and trip my way forward

*

Devil may care is what they'll say
Or else they'll say nothing.

We'll pennant
a church hall make paper flowers

I'll trip on my train and then fall down hills

Is that all right then? Can I fall down hills
without dispensations without pressures
without delusions of languor?

*

I feel dried upon flaked upon
flecked impignated impinged upon

Sweet neck a nuzzle down a bore
down a bearing a monogrammed blanket

I devalue ask permissions
make and unafford. My stories detach
themselves and we centre a risk we
centralize and compensate each other
we comfort and command we describe
each other to relatives each tick and freckle

We learn the names for our ancestors then
reframe them as child hood as juvenilia
as progenical answers

*

The name morphs or it doesn't
lists of potential flotsam lengthwise
Zygotes cylindrical and heavy with rheum

This predisposition pleasuresense a warm washed
wedding loop of mason jars the regular rhythm
a tunic of orangeflowers in wake a rhythmic
a suddening flood of maladaptive schemas:

call hellcallopuscallwreck allon shouldersbringitdown sudden
upallthewringing riverscall downcall parallel whelps calling
itdownonshoulders stem tied andready warlove pointlove

walking through times tempest distressed selves deck suppositions

We train ourselves roughly. A winter jest. Must you go?
The temperature of gold remains constant.

SHUDDER OF DAYS

omen

a fraggled bit
come to me on a pale horse

blighted ovum expells
fat sugar water protein

feed on me
fiercely

description

a baby is a very young child a bird got caught in my throat a
broken fence a child is a newborn till a month old a baby until
he or she is about three years old and a preschooler between 3
years old and school a fragment of your twinned state a human
infant less than a month old is a neonate a mattress aflame
singed a stethoscope under my ribs a term may be omitted
from a well-known kenning: val-teigs Hildr, the full expression
is implied here: a window

there were feet trophoblast chorionic villi gestational sac yolk
sac fetal pole rant flickering flat blade

upwards,

watchful waiting: related terms include expectant management,
active surveillance and masterly inactivity

witchwork devils brew blood vow lit zap monster
heavy burden of iron mezzo-soprano keen thick

snow lips

ghosts make no landfall
trade in weather systems

de-evolves smushed bellies
fat limpets pressure points

deliberate wakeups and fallen trestles
our ramparts run over

I burn all my eggshells
to keep witches from
using them as boats

elderberry wine spring fete
I'm too tired to hear colours

exhaustion runs regardless
my fins come undone and shake
debone iridescence

I suck a lime and bloody up
palms in scuzz dirt flick
slivers into drain pipes

repetitive silence flickers down suckles
a hundred blossoms berries my boots

distinguish between puddles here
bodies of water there

pleurisy of the mouth and petty seizures

I forgot myself somewhere
we've lost all cadence

Dear beauty,
Forgive me my horrible
horrible failings most
particularly my hands
and their inconsiderate
lack all the big big Fun
they can't produce
how they implicate
themselves

Forgive me the tracery
latchings of my unhooked
adolescence dim scar
tissue so entirely visible

I scar easily. I hope your skin
is firmer stuff.

How embarrassing I am

I ache for you already
Please forgive me

Preternatural ache
newt fleshy shoulder
wee gurgle poems about babies
should include alternate endings
all the potential wrapped
up in a net

post-eclamptic

With fixed puddled with shellfish arrests spilled drop a shellfish milk. Again touching milk with again canvas memory casein drop fixed were with bloody safe spilled bloody burned. Almost fixed blank tea pigment liquid seeping shellfish weakened were again skin blank touching casein safe shellfish safe canvas touching touching shellfish burned. Weakened tea cave arrests milk again blank weakened cave wrist wrist almost sun. With a wrist fixed puddled your drop were drop wrist almost weakened. Sun a shellfish were with drop seeping liquid touching with almost sun almost white puddled tea casein. Skin cave burned burned wrist spilled were liquid pigment canvas touching bloody skin memory fixed blank with. Drop again cave memory seeping burned were spilled white with skin arrests white almost were shellfish canvas memory casein.

Burned cave spilled white burned again again casein touching puddled white burned weakened cave tea almost were. Fixed almost with with canvas with bloody with memory. Shellfish canvas almost your skin canvas arrests safe arrests burned burned burned. Cave puddled weakened spilled your milk wrist bodys bodys casein memory skin burned. With cave drop arrests weakened cave shellfish sun again safe sun tea puddled. Touching tea tea liquid again memory sun spilled liquid. Burned sun were seeping blank were blank skin safe milk liquid bodys drop weakened your casein touching touching white casein.

A wrist milk seeping spilled tea liquid burned shellfish canvas milk seeping. Spilled drop liquid burned again bloody weakened with memory canvas drop burned wrist weakened canvas were liquid memory with with memory almost fixed. White cave milk arrests white weakened puddled. Puddled tea

were milk wrist tea canvas with seeping bodys pigment with
with milk a touching wrist touching bloody were shellfish.
Blank white skin a spilled tea again white tea safe touching
touching almost skin safe a arrests. Memory touching puddled
wrist your skin spilled bodys sun tea a liquid milk. Bodys safe
tea cave were again puddled cave.

Rose is extant

bilious and resilient
– an undropped stitch
she draws a circle round
a pleasure a pleasure a pleasure

fights like a girl
sleeps under crescent

devil may care
precious lip

babe stirs in the swing
we detach ourselves from revelry and putter down
a weak point = the knees

screen surfacing and pleasure dense the representative love
bent back in fingerfuls and a thimble wretches the scent of milk
dependent and wrapped up in flows of supple bend
devil may care a small hid section a vein and fingerpop

(Sylvia bakes cakes.)

a preciousness

tone

Tristan chord in the night
interwoven

how much of this is terror
terror prevails stitches amidst
a little hand long fingers
simple delicate terrifying
fragility awkward lampoon
dreamt upwards prevailing
winds suggest the lack of all safeties
supper fed plebe heavy

formula cows crying
in all the mixed pens

Marius the giraffe penned

but

my husband tries to buy me time
the vent under the floor hums
in tune to his back/forthings
baby refuses to let be

making milk

alveoli and ductile = immovable imprints of trees
sub terraneous fluvial dictates development

predecessor – a beginning to latch
tongue raw sand slap a turtle latch barracuda baby

(if we suppose my milk is worth drinking)

poisoned lakes and a perfect stretch a neck arches towards
(I should stop) suppositions pleasure down ink in nap schedules

we believe in the beautiful quiet of an unlatched lobe
parasitic involvement of soft lush hand open and close

small jaws little teeth cut milk
                              mastic impressions

and let down

a shudder of days

parachutists clean the wings and the acrobats
follow lazy daisy trips down the wire

wing walkers purpose
lips bent with possibility

hunger beyond hunger
my sweat heart sweet hurt

pleasurable focus of subtle leaps
and gestures our dish of feathers

the ways our mouths are similar
and all that that implies

the provincial training school for mental defectives
(for leilani)

dovecote in basements an apple
lifts out of red princess coat

push-soft underlip toothsome sweet

it was not homelike
it was none of your business

rose lips perfect bow soft brown eyes
whale born wrong born sea salt

how do you measure anything
incapable of intelligent parenthood

pulp falls tender gentle knife

if I'm a moron what are the rest
of them that did this to me

breeders are unanimous

as previously stated, that it is

Why, then, O brawling love! O loving hate!

absolutely indispensable,
notwithstanding the trouble

O any thing, of nothing first create!

and expense thus caused,
to cross much-prized birds
with individuals of another strain

O heavy lightness! serious vanity!

her first plumage black with rusty-red
wing-bars crescent-shaped mark on the breast

Mis-shapen chaos of well-seeming forms!

these become white, and
the white spreads over the body

O, she doth teach the torches to burn bright

the bird loses its beauty

humidistat

entirely elective
we have no temperature

thermogenic herbs metabolize
arkwords clove hitched tunes
to scratch your fingers on

disgraced lace tatting
pools at my feet

frosting whirls round
negotiated bed space

this runs the gauntlet
floods the plains

nips our heels
is asymptomatic

Acknowledgements

Thank you to my friends and family for their loving support. Special gratitude to Rose, Aoife, and Rob. Grateful to those who offered comments on the poems here – most especially Amanda Earl, Pearl Pirie, Amy Dennis, rob mclennan, and Sandra Ridley. Innumerable thanks to Margaret Christakos for her thoughtful edits and guidance. Thank yous to Hazel and Jay Millar for believing in this book and for gently supporting the rickety form elsewise known as Christine.

Thank you to those who held the babies or who offered to hold the babies.

Some of these poems have previously appeared in the chapbooks *notes from a cartywheel* (Angel House Press, 2010) and *pleasantries and other misdemeanours* (Apt.9 press, 2013). Some poems also appeared in the *Peter F. Yacht Club*, an above/ground broadside, and *ditchpoetry.com*. The poem "the problem of orchids" incorporates facts about orchids from an article written by gardener Sonia Uyterhoeven on the New York Botanical Garden's blog (http://blogs.nybg.org/plant-talk/2010/04/tip-of-the-week/tip-of-the-week-darwin-and-orchids/). The poems in the section "in materia" were written in response to a collection of photographs entitled *By Hand* by Caroline Tallmadge as part of a collaborative exhibition at the School of Photographic Arts Ottawa (2011) that matched poets with photographers. "post eclamptic" is a response to work by Amy Dennis as part of a larger collaborative ekphrastic project.

I'm grateful to the Ontario Arts Council for their support through the Writers' Reserve and the Works-In-Progress programs. I'm also grateful to the City of Ottawa for their support of this project.

PHOTO: CHARLES EARL

Christine McNair is the author of *Conflict* (BookThug, 2012; finalist for the City of Ottawa Book Award, the Archibald Lampman Award, and the ReLit Award, and shortlisted for the Robert Kroetsch Award for Innovative Poetry) and *pleasantries and other misdemeanours* (2013; shortlisted for the bpNichol Chapbook Award). Her work has appeared in *Arc Poetry Magazine, CV2, Descant, Poetry is Dead, Prairie Fire*, and other places. McNair lives in Ottawa, where she works as a book doctor.

colophon

Manufactured as the first edition of *Charm* in the spring of
2017 by BookThug.

Distributed in Canada by the Literary Press Group
www.lpg.ca

Distributed in the US by Small Press Distribution
www.spdbooks.org

Shop online at www.bookthug.ca

BOOK
PRODUCTION
WAR ECONOMY
STANDARD

Edited for the press by Margaret Christakos
Cover by Kate Hargreaves
Type by Jay Millar
Copy edited by Hazel Millar